??? What is Gratitude?

Gratitude is the feeling of thankfulness we have when someone gives us a present, helps, or encourages us with words.

Why keep a gratitude journal?

When you write in your journal, you have the chance to think about all of the things that you are thankful for.

This is how we practice gratitude!

We can be thankful for big things, small things and anything between.

My name is .....

And I am .....

I am ... years old!

My favorite:

Color:

Book:

Food:

Animal:

Sport:

Animated Movie:

Song:

Place to go:

Toy:

Date:

Today I am grateful for...

1) ....

2) ....

3) ....

4) ....

5) ....

I am ...

Beautiful!

Unique!

Blessed!

This person brought me joy today ....

What was the best part about your day?
Draw or write about it...

I Feel...

Happy	Worried	Sad	Angry	Bored

Date:

Today I am grateful for...

1) ....
2) ....
3) ....
4) ....
5) ....

I am ...
Beautiful!
Unique!
Blessed!

This person brought me joy today ....

What was the best part about your day?
Draw or write about it...

I Feel...

Happy  Worried  Sad  Angry  Bored 

Date:

Today I am grateful for...

1) ....

2) ....

3) ....

4) ....

5) ....

I am ...

Beautiful!

Unique!

Blessed!

This person brought me joy today ....

What was the best part about your day?
Draw or write about it...

I Feel...

Happy	Worried	Sad	Angry	Bored

Date:

Today I am grateful for...

1) ....

2) ....

3) ....

4) ....

5) ....

I am ...

Beautiful!

Unique!

Blessed!

This person brought me joy today ....

What was the best part about your day?
Draw or write about it...

I Feel...

Happy	Worried	Sad	Angry	Bored

Date:

Today I am grateful for...

1) ....
2) ....
3) ....
4) ....
5) ....

I am ...

Beautiful!

Unique!

Blessed!

This person brought me joy today ....

What was the best part about your day?
Draw or write about it...

I Feel...

Happy	Worried	Sad	Angry	Bored

Date:

Today I am grateful for...

1) ....

2) ....

3) ....

4) ....

5) ....

I am ...

Beautiful!

Unique!

Blessed!

This person brought me joy today ....

What was the best part about your day?
Draw or write about it...

I Feel...

Happy

Worried

Sad

Angry

Bored

Date:

Today I am grateful for...

1) ....

2) ....

3) ....

4) ....

5) ....

I am ...

Beautiful!

Unique!

Blessed!

This person brought me joy today ....

What was the best part about your day?
Draw or write about it...

I Feel...

Happy	Worried	Sad	Angry	Bored

Date:

Today I am grateful for...

1) ....

2) ....

3) ....

4) ....

5) ....

I am ...

Beautiful!

Unique!

Blessed!

This person brought me joy today ....

What was the best part about your day?
Draw or write about it...

Happy Worried Sad Angry Bored

Date:

Today I am grateful for...

1) ....
2) ....
3) ....
4) ....
5) ....

I am ...
Beautiful!
Unique!
Blessed!

This person brought me joy today ....

What was the best part about your day?
Draw or write about it...

I Feel...

Happy

Worried

Sad

Angry

Bored

Date:

Today I am grateful for...

1) ....
2) ....
3) ....
4) ....
5) ....

I am ...

Beautiful!

Unique!

Blessed!

This person brought me joy today ....

What was the best part about your day?
Draw or write about it...

I Feel...

Happy	Worried	Sad	Angry	Bored

Date:

Today I am grateful for...

1) ....

2) ....

3) ....

4) ....

5) ....

I am ...

Beautiful!

Unique!

Blessed!

This person brought me joy today ....

What was the best part about your day?
Draw or write about it...

I Feel...

Happy

Worried

Sad

Angry

Bored

Date:

Today I am grateful for...

1) ....
2) ....
3) ....
4) ....
5) ....

I am ...

Beautiful!

Unique!

Blessed!

This person brought me joy today ....

What was the best part about your day?
Draw or write about it...

I Feel...

Happy 

Worried 

Sad 

Angry 

Bored 

Date:

Today I am grateful for...

1) ....

2) ....

3) ....

4) ....

5) ....

I am ...

Beautiful!

Unique!

Blessed!

This person brought me joy today ....

What was the best part about your day?
Draw or write about it...

I Feel...

Happy

Worried

Sad

Angry

Bored

Date:

Today I am grateful for...

1) ....

2) ....

3) ....

4) ....

5) ....

I am ...

Beautiful!

Unique!

Blessed!

This person brought me joy today ....

What was the best part about your day?
Draw or write about it...

I Feel...

Happy

Worried

Sad

Angry

Bored

Date:

Today I am grateful for...

1) ....
2) ....
3) ....
4) ....
5) ....

I am ...

Beautiful!

Unique!

Blessed!

This person brought me joy today ....

What was the best part about your day?
Draw or write about it...

I Feel...

Happy

Worried

Sad

Angry

Bored

Date:

Today I am grateful for...

1) ....

2) ....

3) ....

4) ....

5) ....

I am ...

Beautiful!

Unique!

Blessed!

This person brought me joy today ....

What was the best part about your day?
Draw or write about it...

I Feel...

Happy

Worried

Sad

Angry

Bored

Date:

Today I am grateful for...

1) ....

2) ....

3) ....

4) ....

5) ....

I am ...

Beautiful!

Unique!

Blessed!

This person brought me joy today ....

What was the best part about your day?
Draw or write about it...

I Feel...

Happy	Worried	Sad	Angry	Bored

Date:

Today I am grateful for...

1) ....

2) ....

3) ....

4) ....

5) ....

I am ...

Beautiful!

Unique!

Blessed!

This person brought me joy today ....

What was the best part about your day?
Draw or write about it...

I Feel...

Happy	Worried	Sad	Angry	Bored

Date:

Today I am grateful for...

1) ....

2) ....

3) ....

4) ....

5) ....

I am ...

Beautiful!

Unique!

Blessed!

This person brought me joy today ....

What was the best part about your day?
Draw or write about it...

I Feel...

Happy

Worried

Sad

Angry

Bored

Date:

Today I am grateful for...

1) ....

2) ....

3) ....

4) ....

5) ....

I am ...

Beautiful!

Unique!

Blessed!

This person brought me joy today ....

What was the best part about your day?
Draw or write about it...

I Feel...

Happy

Worried

Sad

Angry

Bored

Date:

Today I am grateful for...

1) ....

2) ....

3) ....

4) ....

5) ....

I am ...

Beautiful!

Unique!

Blessed!

This person brought me joy today ....

What was the best part about your day?
Draw or write about it...

I Feel...

Happy	Worried	Sad	Angry	Bored

Date:

Today I am grateful for...

1) ....
2) ....
3) ....
4) ....
5) ....

I am ...

Beautiful!

Unique!

Blessed!

This person brought me joy today ....

What was the best part about your day?
Draw or write about it...

I Feel...

Happy 

Worried 

Sad 

Angry 

Bored 

Date:

Today I am grateful for...

1) ....

2) ....

3) ....

4) ....

5) ....

I am ...

Beautiful!

Unique!

Blessed!

This person brought me joy today ....

What was the best part about your day?
Draw or write about it...

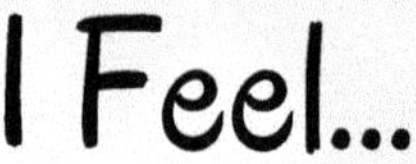

Happy	Worried	Sad	Angry	Bored

Date:

Today I am grateful for...

1) ....
2) ....
3) ....
4) ....
5) ....

I am ...

Beautiful!

Unique!

Blessed!

This person brought me joy today ....

What was the best part about your day?
Draw or write about it...

I Feel...

Happy	Worried	Sad	Angry	Bored

Date:

Today I am grateful for...

1) ....

2) ....

3) ....

4) ....

5) ....

I am ...

Beautiful!

Unique!

Blessed!

This person brought me joy today ....

What was the best part about your day?
Draw or write about it...

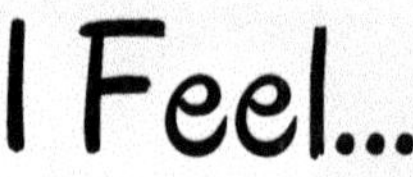

I Feel...

Happy	Worried	Sad	Angry	Bored

Date:

Today I am grateful for...

1) ....

2) ....

3) ....

4) ....

5) ....

I am ...

Beautiful!

Unique!

Blessed!

This person brought me joy today ....

What was the best part about your day?
Draw or write about it...

I Feel...

Happy · Worried · Sad · Angry · Bored

Date:

Today I am grateful for...

1) ....

2) ....

3) ....

4) ....

5) ....

I am ...

Beautiful!

Unique!

Blessed!

This person brought me joy today ....

What was the best part about your day?
Draw or write about it...

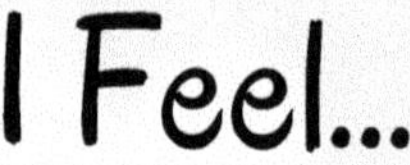

Happy	Worried	Sad	Angry	Bored

Date:

Today I am grateful for...

1) ....

2) ....

3) ....

4) ....

5) ....

I am ...

Beautiful!

Unique!

Blessed!

This person brought me joy today ....

What was the best part about your day?
Draw or write about it...

I Feel...

Happy Worried Sad Angry Bored

Date:

Today I am grateful for...

1) ....
2) ....
3) ....
4) ....
5) ....

I am ...

Beautiful!

Unique!

Blessed!

This person brought me joy today ....

What was the best part about your day?
Draw or write about it...

I Feel...

Happy

Worried

Sad

Angry

Bored

Date:

Today I am grateful for...

1) ....

2) ....

3) ....

4) ....

5) ....

I am ...

Beautiful!

Unique!

Blessed!

This person brought me joy today ....

What was the best part about your day?
Draw or write about it...

I Feel...

Happy

Worried

Sad

Angry

Bored

Date:

Today I am grateful for...

1) ....

2) ....

3) ....

4) ....

5) ....

I am ...

Beautiful!

Unique!

Blessed!

This person brought me joy today ....

What was the best part about your day?
Draw or write about it...

I Feel...

Happy

Worried

Sad

Angry

Bored

Date:

Today I am grateful for...

1) ....
2) ....
3) ....
4) ....
5) ....

I am ...

Beautiful!

Unique!

Blessed!

This person brought me joy today ....

What was the best part about your day?
Draw or write about it...

I Feel...

Happy	Worried	Sad	Angry	Bored

Date:

Today I am grateful for...

1) ....
2) ....
3) ....
4) ....
5) ....

I am ...

Beautiful!

Unique!

Blessed!

This person brought me joy today ....

What was the best part about your day?
Draw or write about it...

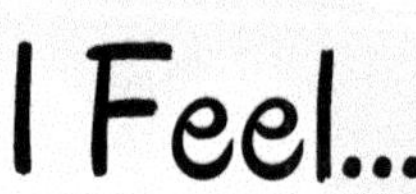

I Feel...

Happy

Worried

Sad

Angry

Bored

Date:

Today I am grateful for...

1) ....

2) ....

3) ....

4) ....

5) ....

I am ...

Beautiful!

Unique!

Blessed!

This person brought me joy today ....

What was the best part about your day?
Draw or write about it...

I Feel...

Happy

Worried

Sad

Angry

Bored

Date:

Today I am grateful for...

1) ....

2) ....

3) ....

4) ....

5) ....

I am ...

Beautiful!

Unique!

Blessed!

This person brought me joy today ....

What was the best part about your day?
Draw or write about it...

Happy	Worried	Sad	Angry	Bored

Date:

Today I am grateful for...

1) ....

2) ....

3) ....

4) ....

5) ....

I am ...

Beautiful!

Unique!

Blessed!

This person brought me joy today ....

What was the best part about your day?
Draw or write about it...

I Feel...

Happy

Worried

Sad

Angry

Bored

Date:

Today I am grateful for...

1) ....

2) ....

3) ....

4) ....

5) ....

I am ...

Beautiful!

Unique!

Blessed!

This person brought me joy today ....

What was the best part about your day?
Draw or write about it...

I Feel...

Happy	Worried	Sad	Angry	Bored

Date:

Today I am grateful for...

1) ....
2) ....
3) ....
4) ....
5) ....

I am ...

Beautiful!

Unique!

Blessed!

This person brought me joy today ....

What was the best part about your day?
Draw or write about it...

I Feel...

Happy

Worried

Sad

Angry

Bored

Date:

Today I am grateful for...

1) ....
2) ....
3) ....
4) ....
5) ....

I am ...

Beautiful!

Unique!

Blessed!

This person brought me joy today ....

What was the best part about your day?
Draw or write about it...

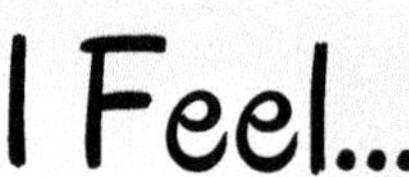

I Feel...

Happy	Worried	Sad	Angry	Bored

Date:

Today I am grateful for...

1) ....
2) ....
3) ....
4) ....
5) ....

I am ...

Beautiful!

Unique!

Blessed!

This person brought me joy today ....

What was the best part about your day?
Draw or write about it...

I Feel...

Happy

Worried

Sad

Angry

Bored

Date:

Today I am grateful for...

1) ....
2) ....
3) ....
4) ....
5) ....

I am ...

Beautiful!

Unique!

Blessed!

This person brought me joy today ....

What was the best part about your day?
Draw or write about it...

I Feel...

Happy

Worried

Sad

Angry

Bored

Date:

Today I am grateful for...

1) ....

2) ....

3) ....

4) ....

5) ....

I am ...

Beautiful!

Unique!

Blessed!

This person brought me joy today ....

What was the best part about your day?
Draw or write about it...

I Feel...

Happy	Worried	Sad	Angry	Bored

Date:

Today I am grateful for...

1) ....

2) ....

3) ....

4) ....

5) ....

I am ...

Beautiful!

Unique!

Blessed!

This person brought me joy today ....

What was the best part about your day?
Draw or write about it...

Happy	Worried	Sad	Angry	Bored

Date:

Today I am grateful for...

1) ....
2) ....
3) ....
4) ....
5) ....

I am ...

Beautiful!

Unique!

Blessed!

This person brought me joy today ....

What was the best part about your day?
Draw or write about it...

I Feel...

Happy

Worried

Sad

Angry

Bored

Date:

Today I am grateful for...

1) ....

2) ....

3) ....

4) ....

5) ....

I am ...

Beautiful!

Unique!

Blessed!

This person brought me joy today ....

What was the best part about your day?
Draw or write about it...

I Feel...

Happy	Worried	Sad	Angry	Bored

Date:

Today I am grateful for...

1) ....
2) ....
3) ....
4) ....
5) ....

I am ...

Beautiful!

Unique!

Blessed!

This person brought me joy today ....

What was the best part about your day?
Draw or write about it...

I Feel...

Happy

Worried

Sad

Angry

Bored

Date:

Today I am grateful for...

1) ....
2) ....
3) ....
4) ....
5) ....

I am ...

Beautiful!

Unique!

Blessed!

This person brought me joy today ....

What was the best part about your day?
Draw or write about it...

I Feel...

Happy

Worried

Sad

Angry

Bored

Date:

Today I am grateful for...

1) ....
2) ....
3) ....
4) ....
5) ....

I am ...

Beautiful!

Unique!

Blessed!

This person brought me joy today ....

What was the best part about your day?
Draw or write about it...

I Feel...

Happy

Worried

Sad

Angry

Bored

Date:

Today I am grateful for...

1) ....

2) ....

3) ....

4) ....

5) ....

I am ...

Beautiful!

Unique!

Blessed!

This person brought me joy today ....

What was the best part about your day?
Draw or write about it...

I Feel...

Happy	Worried	Sad	Angry	Bored

Date:

Today I am grateful for...

1) ....

2) ....

3) ....

4) ....

5) ....

I am ...

Beautiful!

Unique!

Blessed!

This person brought me joy today ....

What was the best part about your day?
Draw or write about it...

I Feel...

Happy

Worried

Sad

Angry

Bored

Date:

Today I am grateful for...

1) ....

2) ....

3) ....

4) ....

5) ....

I am ...

Beautiful!

Unique!

Blessed!

This person brought me joy today ....

What was the best part about your day?
Draw or write about it...

I Feel...

Happy Worried Sad Angry Bored

Date:

Today I am grateful for...

1) ....
2) ....
3) ....
4) ....
5) ....

I am ...

Beautiful!

Unique!

Blessed!

This person brought me joy today ....

What was the best part about your day?
Draw or write about it...

I Feel...

Happy 

Worried 

Sad 

Angry 

Bored 

Date:

Today I am grateful for...

1) ....

2) ....

3) ....

4) ....

5) ....

I am ...

Beautiful!

Unique!

Blessed!

This person brought me joy today ....

What was the best part about your day?
Draw or write about it...

I Feel...

Happy	Worried	Sad	Angry	Bored

Date:

Today I am grateful for...

1) ....

2) ....

3) ....

4) ....

5) ....

I am ...

Beautiful!

Unique!

Blessed!

This person brought me joy today ....

What was the best part about your day?
Draw or write about it...

Happy	Worried	Sad	Angry	Bored

Date:

Today I am grateful for...

1) ....

2) ....

3) ....

4) ....

5) ....

I am ...

Beautiful!

Unique!

Blessed!

This person brought me joy today ....

What was the best part about your day?
Draw or write about it...

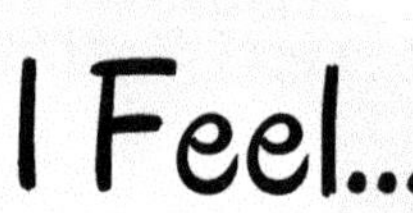

Happy Worried Sad Angry Bored

Date:

Today I am grateful for...

1) ....
2) ....
3) ....
4) ....
5) ....

I am ...

Beautiful!

Unique!

Blessed!

This person brought me joy today ....

What was the best part about your day?
Draw or write about it...

I Feel...

Happy	Worried	Sad	Angry	Bored

Date:

Today I am grateful for...

1) ....

2) ....

3) ....

4) ....

5) ....

I am ...

Beautiful!

Unique!

Blessed!

This person brought me joy today ....

What was the best part about your day?
Draw or write about it...

I Feel...

Happy

Worried

Sad

Angry

Bored

Date:

Today I am grateful for...

1) ....
2) ....
3) ....
4) ....
5) ....

I am ...

Beautiful!

Unique!

Blessed!

This person brought me joy today ....

What was the best part about your day?
Draw or write about it...

I Feel...

Happy

Worried

Sad

Angry

Bored

Date:

Today I am grateful for...

1) ....
2) ....
3) ....
4) ....
5) ....

I am ...

Beautiful!

Unique!

Blessed!

This person brought me joy today ....

What was the best part about your day?
Draw or write about it...

I Feel...

Happy

Worried

Sad

Angry

Bored

Date:

Today I am grateful for...

1) ....

2) ....

3) ....

4) ....

5) ....

I am ...

Beautiful!

Unique!

Blessed!

This person brought me joy today ....

What was the best part about your day?
Draw or write about it...

I Feel...

Happy Worried Sad Angry Bored

Date:

Today I am grateful for...

1) ....

2) ....

3) ....

4) ....

5) ....

I am ...

Beautiful!

Unique!

Blessed!

This person brought me joy today ....

What was the best part about your day?
Draw or write about it...

I Feel...

Happy 

Worried 

Sad 

Angry 

Bored 

Date:

Today I am grateful for...

1) ....

2) ....

3) ....

4) ....

5) ....

I am ...

Beautiful!

Unique!

Blessed!

This person brought me joy today ....

What was the best part about your day?
Draw or write about it...

I Feel...

Happy	Worried	Sad	Angry	Bored

Date:

Today I am grateful for...

1) ....

2) ....

3) ....

4) ....

5) ....

I am ...

Beautiful!

Unique!

Blessed!

This person brought me joy today ....

What was the best part about your day?
Draw or write about it...

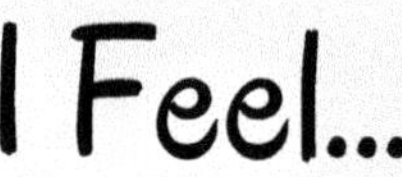

I Feel...

Happy	Worried	Sad	Angry	Bored

Date:

Today I am grateful for...

1) ....
2) ....
3) ....
4) ....
5) ....

I am ...

Beautiful!

Unique!

Blessed!

This person brought me joy today ....

What was the best part about your day?
Draw or write about it...

I Feel...

Happy Worried Sad Angry Bored

Date:

Today I am grateful for...

1) ....
2) ....
3) ....
4) ....
5) ....

I am ...

Beautiful!

Unique!

Blessed!

This person brought me joy today ....

What was the best part about your day?
Draw or write about it...

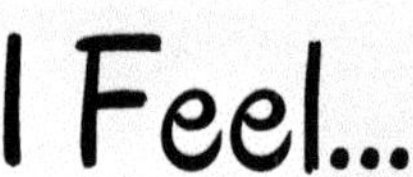

I Feel...

Happy	Worried	Sad	Angry	Bored

Date:

Today I am grateful for...

1) ....

2) ....

3) ....

4) ....

5) ....

I am ...

Beautiful!

Unique!

Blessed!

This person brought me joy today ....

What was the best part about your day?
Draw or write about it...

I Feel...

Happy	Worried	Sad	Angry	Bored

Date:

Today I am grateful for...

1) ....

2) ....

3) ....

4) ....

5) ....

I am ...

Beautiful!

Unique!

Blessed!

This person brought me joy today ....

What was the best part about your day?
Draw or write about it...

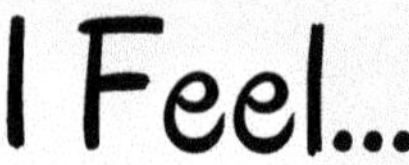

I Feel...

Happy	Worried	Sad	Angry	Bored

Date:

Today I am grateful for...

1) ....

2) ....

3) ....

4) ....

5) ....

I am ...

Beautiful!

Unique!

Blessed!

This person brought me joy today ....

What was the best part about your day?
Draw or write about it...

I Feel...

Happy

Worried

Sad

Angry

Bored

Date:

Today I am grateful for...

1) ....
2) ....
3) ....
4) ....
5) ....

I am ...

Beautiful!

Unique!

Blessed!

This person brought me joy today ....

What was the best part about your day?
Draw or write about it...

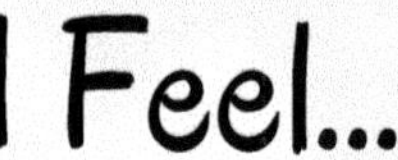

I Feel...

Happy	Worried	Sad	Angry	Bored

Date:

Today I am grateful for...

1) ....

2) ....

3) ....

4) ....

5) ....

I am ...

Beautiful!

Unique!

Blessed!

This person brought me joy today ....

What was the best part about your day?
Draw or write about it...

I Feel...

Happy Worried Sad Angry Bored

Date:

Today I am grateful for...

1) ....
2) ....
3) ....
4) ....
5) ....

I am ...

Beautiful!

Unique!

Blessed!

This person brought me joy today ....

What was the best part about your day?
Draw or write about it...

I Feel...

Happy

Worried

Sad

Angry

Bored

Date:

Today I am grateful for...

1) ....

2) ....

3) ....

4) ....

5) ....

I am ...

Beautiful!

Unique!

Blessed!

This person brought me joy today ....

What was the best part about your day?
Draw or write about it...

I Feel...

Happy

Worried

Sad

Angry

Bored

Date:

Today I am grateful for...

1) ....

2) ....

3) ....

4) ....

5) ....

I am ...

Beautiful!

Unique!

Blessed!

This person brought me joy today ....

What was the best part about your day?
Draw or write about it...

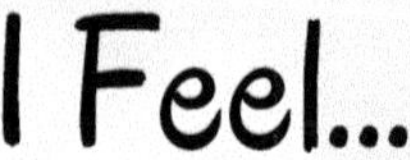

Happy	Worried	Sad	Angry	Bored

Date:

Today I am grateful for...

1) ....

2) ....

3) ....

4) ....

5) ....

I am ...

Beautiful!

Unique!

Blessed!

This person brought me joy today ....

What was the best part about your day?
Draw or write about it...

Happy	Worried	Sad	Angry	Bored

Date:

Today I am grateful for...

1) ....

2) ....

3) ....

4) ....

5) ....

I am ...

Beautiful!

Unique!

Blessed!

This person brought me joy today ....

What was the best part about your day?
Draw or write about it...

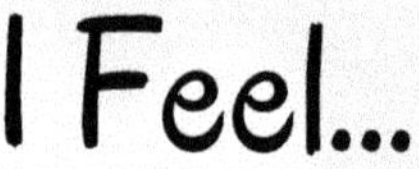

Happy Worried Sad Angry Bored

Date:

Today I am grateful for...

1) ....
2) ....
3) ....
4) ....
5) ....

I am ...

Beautiful!

Unique!

Blessed!

This person brought me joy today ....

What was the best part about your day?
Draw or write about it...

I Feel...

Happy	Worried	Sad	Angry	Bored

Date:

Today I am grateful for...

1) ....
2) ....
3) ....
4) ....
5) ....

I am ...

Beautiful!

Unique!

Blessed!

This person brought me joy today ....

What was the best part about your day?
Draw or write about it...

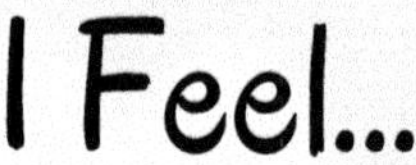

Happy	Worried	Sad	Angry	Bored

Date:

Today I am grateful for...

1) ....

2) ....

3) ....

4) ....

5) ....

I am ...

Beautiful!

Unique!

Blessed!

This person brought me joy today ....

What was the best part about your day?
Draw or write about it...

I Feel...

Happy

Worried

Sad

Angry

Bored

Date:

Today I am grateful for...

1) ....

2) ....

3) ....

4) ....

5) ....

I am ...

Beautiful!

Unique!

Blessed!

This person brought me joy today ....

What was the best part about your day?
Draw or write about it...

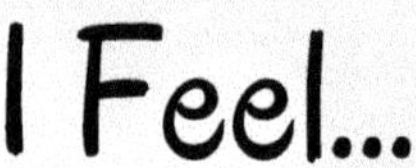

I Feel...

Happy

Worried

Sad

Angry

Bored

Date:

Today I am grateful for...

1) ....

2) ....

3) ....

4) ....

5) ....

I am ...

Beautiful!

Unique!

Blessed!

This person brought me joy today ....

What was the best part about your day?
Draw or write about it...

I Feel...

Happy

Worried

Sad

Angry

Bored

Date:

Today I am grateful for...

1) ....

2) ....

3) ....

4) ....

5) ....

I am ...

Beautiful!

Unique!

Blessed!

This person brought me joy today ....

What was the best part about your day?
Draw or write about it...

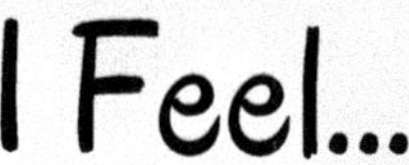

I Feel...

Happy	Worried	Sad	Angry	Bored

Date:

Today I am grateful for...

1) ....
2) ....
3) ....
4) ....
5) ....

I am ...

Beautiful!

Unique!

Blessed!

This person brought me joy today ....

What was the best part about your day?
Draw or write about it...

I Feel...

Happy	Worried	Sad	Angry	Bored

Date:

Today I am grateful for...

1) ....

2) ....

3) ....

4) ....

5) ....

I am ...

Beautiful!

Unique!

Blessed!

This person brought me joy today ....

What was the best part about your day?
Draw or write about it...

I Feel...

Happy

Worried

Sad

Angry

Bored

Date:

Today I am grateful for...

1) ....
2) ....
3) ....
4) ....
5) ....

I am ...

Beautiful!

Unique!

Blessed!

This person brought me joy today ....

What was the best part about your day?
Draw or write about it...

Happy	Worried	Sad	Angry	Bored

Date:

Today I am grateful for...

1) ....

2) ....

3) ....

4) ....

5) ....

I am ...

Beautiful!

Unique!

Blessed!

This person brought me joy today ....

What was the best part about your day?
Draw or write about it...

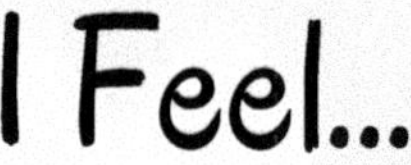

Happy	Worried	Sad	Angry	Bored

Date:

Today I am grateful for...

1) ....
2) ....
3) ....
4) ....
5) ....

I am ...

Beautiful!

Unique!

Blessed!

This person brought me joy today ....

What was the best part about your day?
Draw or write about it...

I Feel...

Happy 

Worried 

Sad 

Angry 

Bored 

Date:

Today I am grateful for...

1) ....
2) ....
3) ....
4) ....
5) ....

I am ...

Beautiful!

Unique!

Blessed!

This person brought me joy today ....

What was the best part about your day?
Draw or write about it...

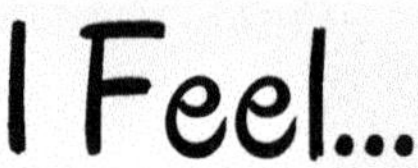

Happy	Worried	Sad	Angry	Bored

Date:

Today I am grateful for...

1) ....

2) ....

3) ....

4) ....

5) ....

I am ...

Beautiful!

Unique!

Blessed!

This person brought me joy today ....

What was the best part about your day?
Draw or write about it...

I Feel...

Happy

Worried

Sad

Angry

Bored

Date:

Today I am grateful for...

1) ....

2) ....

3) ....

4) ....

5) ....

I am ...

Beautiful!

Unique!

Blessed!

This person brought me joy today ....

What was the best part about your day?
Draw or write about it...

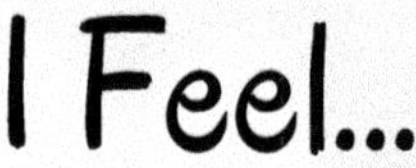

Happy Worried Sad Angry Bored

Date:

Today I am grateful for...

1) ....
2) ....
3) ....
4) ....
5) ....

I am ...

Beautiful!

Unique!

Blessed!

This person brought me joy today ....

What was the best part about your day?
Draw or write about it...

I Feel...

Happy

Worried

Sad

Angry

Bored

Date:

Today I am grateful for...

1) ....

2) ....

3) ....

4) ....

5) ....

I am ...

Beautiful!

Unique!

Blessed!

This person brought me joy today ....

What was the best part about your day?
Draw or write about it...

I Feel...

Happy	Worried	Sad	Angry	Bored

Date:

Today I am grateful for...

1) ....

2) ....

3) ....

4) ....

5) ....

I am ...

Beautiful!

Unique!

Blessed!

This person brought me joy today ....

What was the best part about your day?
Draw or write about it...

I Feel...

Happy

Worried

Sad

Angry

Bored

Date:

Today I am grateful for...

1) ....
2) ....
3) ....
4) ....
5) ....

I am ...

Beautiful!

Unique!

Blessed!

This person brought me joy today ....

What was the best part about your day?
Draw or write about it...

I Feel...

Happy

Worried

Sad

Angry

Bored

Date:

Today I am grateful for...

1) ....

2) ....

3) ....

4) ....

5) ....

I am ...

Beautiful!

Unique!

Blessed!

This person brought me joy today ....

What was the best part about your day?
Draw or write about it...

I Feel...

Happy	Worried	Sad	Angry	Bored

Date:

Today I am grateful for...

1) ....
2) ....
3) ....
4) ....
5) ....

I am ...

Beautiful!

Unique!

Blessed!

This person brought me joy today ....

What was the best part about your day?
Draw or write about it...

I Feel...

Happy	Worried	Sad	Angry	Bored

Date:

Today I am grateful for...

1) ....
2) ....
3) ....
4) ....
5) ....

I am ...

Beautiful!

Unique!

Blessed!

This person brought me joy today ....

What was the best part about your day?
Draw or write about it...

I Feel...

Happy

Worried

Sad

Angry

Bored

Date:

Today I am grateful for...

1) ....

2) ....

3) ....

4) ....

5) ....

I am ...

Beautiful!

Unique!

Blessed!

This person brought me joy today ....

What was the best part about your day?
Draw or write about it...

I Feel...

Happy

Worried

Sad

Angry

Bored

Date:

Today I am grateful for...

1) ....
2) ....
3) ....
4) ....
5) ....

I am ...

Beautiful!

Unique!

Blessed!

This person brought me joy today ....

What was the best part about your day?
Draw or write about it...

I Feel...

Happy	Worried	Sad	Angry	Bored

Date:

Today I am grateful for...

1) ....
2) ....
3) ....
4) ....
5) ....

I am ...

Beautiful!

Unique!

Blessed!

This person brought me joy today ....

What was the best part about your day?
Draw or write about it...

I Feel...

Happy 

Worried 

Sad 

Angry 

Bored 

Date:

Today I am grateful for...

1) ....

2) ....

3) ....

4) ....

5) ....

I am ...

Beautiful!

Unique!

Blessed!

This person brought me joy today ....

What was the best part about your day?
Draw or write about it...

I Feel...

Happy	Worried	Sad	Angry	Bored

Date:

Today I am grateful for...

1) ....
2) ....
3) ....
4) ....
5) ....

I am ...
Beautiful!
Unique!
Blessed!

This person brought me joy today ....

What was the best part about your day?
Draw or write about it...

I Feel...

Happy	Worried	Sad	Angry	Bored

Date:

Today I am grateful for...

1) ....
2) ....
3) ....
4) ....
5) ....

I am ...

Beautiful!

Unique!

Blessed!

This person brought me joy today ....

What was the best part about your day?
Draw or write about it...

Happy Worried Sad Angry Bored

Date:

Today I am grateful for...

1) ....

2) ....

3) ....

4) ....

5) ....

I am ...

Beautiful!

Unique!

Blessed!

This person brought me joy today ....

What was the best part about your day?
Draw or write about it...

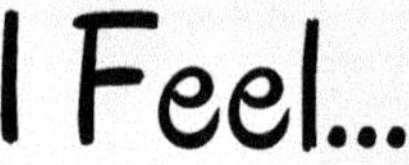

I Feel...

Happy

Worried

Sad

Angry

Bored

Date:

Today I am grateful for...

1) ....

2) ....

3) ....

4) ....

5) ....

I am ...

Beautiful!

Unique!

Blessed!

This person brought me joy today ....

What was the best part about your day?
Draw or write about it...

I Feel...

Happy

Worried

Sad

Angry

Bored

Date:

Today I am grateful for...

1) ....

2) ....

3) ....

4) ....

5) ....

I am ...

Beautiful!

Unique!

Blessed!

This person brought me joy today ....

What was the best part about your day?
Draw or write about it...

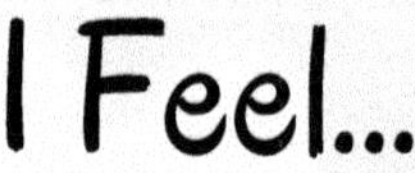

I Feel...

Happy

Worried

Sad

Angry

Bored

Date:

Today I am grateful for...

1) ....

2) ....

3) ....

4) ....

5) ....

I am ...

Beautiful!

Unique!

Blessed!

This person brought me joy today ....

What was the best part about your day?
Draw or write about it...

I Feel...

Happy	Worried	Sad	Angry	Bored

Date:

Today I am grateful for...

1) ....
2) ....
3) ....
4) ....
5) ....

I am ...
Beautiful!
Unique!
Blessed!

This person brought me joy today ....

What was the best part about your day?
Draw or write about it...

I Feel...

Happy 

Worried 

Sad 

Angry 

Bored 

Date:

Today I am grateful for...

1) ....

2) ....

3) ....

4) ....

5) ....

I am ...

Beautiful!

Unique!

Blessed!

This person brought me joy today ....

What was the best part about your day?
Draw or write about it...

Happy

Worried

Sad

Angry

Bored

www.ingramcontent.com/pod-product-compliance
Ingram Content Group UK Ltd.
Pitfield, Milton Keynes, MK11 3LW, UK
UKHW051137260726
13967UKWH00010B/3110

9 781291 630213